Can the Federal Bureau of Investigation feed information from political files to employers to get unionists fired from their jobs? Can the Immigration and Naturalization Service deport foreign-born workers for their political views? Can police agencies legally plant stool pigeons in unions and other organizations, even if no one involved is suspected of a crime?

According to the government, the answer is yes. The federal government claims that it has the legal right to spy on, harass, blacklist, and deport those whose political views it disapproves of. It can undertake such secret-police action, the government says, even against individuals and organizations whose political activities are completely legal and supposedly protected by the Bill of Rights.

These assertions have been put forward by the Justice Department in official court documents outlining the defense the government will present in the trial, scheduled to begin March 16, of the lawsuit against the government by the Socialist Workers Party and Young Socialist Alliance. The suit demands a halt to the government's spy operation. And it demands $40 million in damages for years of harassment.

The Justice Department document asserts that "The issue in this case is not whether the SWP, the YSA, or any of their members can be proved guilty of a crime beyond a reasonable doubt. The issue is whether the Government has the right to keep itself informed of the activities of groups that openly advocate revolutionary change in the structure and leadership of the Government of the United States, *even if such advocacy might be within the letter of the law*" (emphasis added).

As is well established, the government's secret police keep

themselves "informed" by such methods as the use of paid informers, illegal wiretaps, burglaries, and other equally unconstitutional methods.

The brazenness with which the government presents its "right" to spy is a shift. Previously it had justified more than forty years of investigating and harassment on the grounds that the SWP was suspected of conducting illegal activity. But they were never able to make this rap stick. In the mid-seventies, both the House and Senate subcommittees investigating activities of the FBI admitted that the FBI, despite forty years of spying, had found no evidence of any illegal activities by the socialists.

Why does the government engage in such activities at all? Isn't it supposed to safeguard the democratic rights of all of us?

The government's violation of democratic rights is not an aberration of a particular president, such as Richard Nixon, nor the excesses of overzealous secret-police officials like J. Edgar Hoover. It flows from the need of the employing class to defend their rule from the vast majority, the working class.

Most of us aren't used to thinking about politics in this way. From the time we are children we are taught that the government represents the "people" or the "national interest." The government, political parties, and news media don't reflect classes, we are told. Insofar as social classes are mentioned, it's usually only to say that there are some poor people on the bottom, a few billionaires on the top, and a vast "middle class," including everyone from auto workers to corporate executives, in between.

But the deepening economic crisis in the U.S. is changing the way many workers look at themselves and at the government. There is growing recognition that the government, as well as the Democratic and Republican parties, are on the side of the employers in driving down the living standards of workers, attacking trade unions, reversing gains made by minorities and women, and preparing for foreign wars.

As more and more workers reject their previous outlook and adopt more radical ideas and more militant forms of struggle, the employers increasingly rely on the repression. There is more frequent use of cops to intimidate striking workers, more use of injunctions to break strikes, more cop murders of Black and Latino youth, and stepped up use of the secret police against the unions, Black organizations, and socialist groups. This in turn serves to encourage racist and fascist scum like the Ku Klux Klan to carry out terrorist attacks.

"Workers' Rights vs. the Secret Police" discusses the SWP and YSA lawsuit and the campaign in support of it in this framework. It is based on a talk presented on behalf of the Political Committee of the SWP at a socialist educational conference in August 1980.

In explaining the new stage in this campaign, which is a result of the deepening economic crisis and the more radical moods in the working class, it was pointed out that "we are experiencing a general step-up in incidents of FBI-type harassment. These are things we haven't seen for a while, including spying and harassment on the job, not just by the FBI and the cops but also by private detective agencies." It did not take long for such incidents to come to light.

Four months after this speech was given, five unionists at the Brooklyn Navy Yard were fired at the instigation of the navy. The sole reason for their dismissal was that they were accused of membership in the Socialist Workers Party.

The five pipefitters returned the following morning and handed out 500 copies of their termination notice to coworkers, with a protest on the back. "How can the U.S. Navy itself claim that the ships we work on are being readied to protect democratic rights abroad when the Navy itself suppresses democratic rights of workers on Navy ships?" the leaflet asked. News of the political firings swept through the yard, and many workers expressed their anger at this violation of fundamental rights. The union began to make inquiries about the justification for the firings.

A political fight is not what the company, the Coastal Dry

Dock and Repair Corporation, had bargained for. It got cold feet. By that evening the fired workers had been rehired. The news was greeted by workers in the Navy Yard as a solid victory that was doubly sweet because it was won against the U.S. Navy as well as the Coastal Dry Dock bosses.

Within weeks after the Navy Yard victory, however, another case of union members being fired for purely political reasons broke. The giant Lockheed corporation, one of the nation's largest war contractors, began firing members of the International Association of Machinists at its Marietta, Georgia, aircraft plant. The unionists were fired because they showed up in Lockheed "security" files as suspected members of the SWP or YSA.

In December and January, fifteen workers were dismissed. All fifteen have been active members of IAM Lodge 709 and were involved in its struggles against speedup and unsafe working conditions in the plant. Most also belong to the SWP.

The security officer who compiled files on the fifteen, known as "FBI Bob" Lang among the workers, spilled the beans when questioned under oath by attorneys for the SWP. Lang admitted that massive surveillance against the union militants began October 20, the day after an SWP election campaign leaflet was distributed outside a union meeting. The leaflet supported the idea of the unions forming a labor party, independent of the Democrats and Republicans. It noted that the September 1980 national convention of the International Association of Machinists had discussed this idea.

The files show that Lockheed has finks report on all union meetings as well as on discussions and activities engaged in by union members on and off the job. The workers who were targeted for firing, as well as some of their co-workers, were followed around the plant, to their homes, to restaurants, on shopping trips, and even to the laundry. Dossiers were compiled on people the socialists talked to, with special attention to Black workers. Information on the workers was collected from police agencies and from the FBI's political dossiers. But FBI Bob's thick files turned up absolutely nothing illegal, violent, or secretive. Today, the fired unionists are waging a nation-wide effort to win their jobs back.

The firings at Lockheed and the Brooklyn Navy Yard are examples of the kind of attacks that increasingly face all working people who struggle for their rights. So it's no wonder that these victimizations are arousing indignation as workers learn about them.

Fired Lockheed workers who have toured the country speaking about their case have received a very warm reception. And dozens of statements of solidarity for the Lockheed workers have been received from unionists.

Scores of union officials and Black organizations have endorsed the SWP and YSA suit against the government, including Douglas Fraser, president of the United Auto Workers.

The capitalists and their government have targeted the SWP and YSA for persecution because our ideas speak to the needs of working people. Workers' rights are not "given" by the capitalist government—they have been won and defended through the mobilization of our class and its allies. The suit of the SWP and YSA against the secret police is part of that struggle.

February 1981

Workers' rights vs. the secret police

This case has a long history, much longer than we usually think of. Like so much of what we in the Socialist Workers Party and the Young Socialist Alliance are involved in today, our fight against the FBI has its roots in the period around 1848, when the modern communist movement began in Europe. That was when the industrial working class first entered the political arena as a class, with a vanguard consciously charting a course in its historic interests. And the ruling classes responded with, among other things, the unleashing of police spies, agents provocateurs, and political frame-ups.

Our fight against the political police today continues the fight waged by Marx and Engels, beginning in 1848, against the series of frame-ups of leaders of the Communist League, including successful defenses of Marx himself. These led up to the notori-

Workers' Rights versus the Secret Police is based on a talk given at a socialist education conference at Oberlin, Ohio, in August 1980. Larry Seigle is author of "Washington's 50 Year Domestic Contra Operation," published in *New International* no. 6, distributed by Pathfinder.

ous Cologne trial in 1852, which took place in the wake of the defeats of the 1848–49 revolutions. All the police methods we see today came to light there: the accusation of illegal conspiracy based solely on political ideas and activities, the false testimony of informers, even "mail covers" and police forgeries. The original "black bag job"—to use a current FBI term—took place in preparation for that frame up.

Our fight today has many parallels with the fight by the German Social Democratic Party against the Anti-Socialist Laws in the last quarter of the nineteenth century. The party fought for the right to function openly, as a legal party. And it refused to begin acting as a conspiratorial society even when forced into illegality.

Our war with the FBI today is in a direct line of descent from the fight that the Bolshevik Party and the entire Russian workers' movement waged against the Okhrana, the tsars' FBI, which fielded an army of informers against the working-class movement. When the Russian workers finally got their hands on these informer files—it took a revolution to do it—they found records of almost 40,000 agents provocateurs. That was the first time in history that the entire account of a secret police operation, including its spy and disruption efforts, fell into the hands of the working class.

Our fight against the political police also has, of course a long tradition in this country. It includes the national campaign against the execution of the Haymarket frame-up victims, the battles against the Pinkertons and other labor-spy outfits, and struggles to stop police and KKK racist terror against Blacks, Mexicanos, and Asians. Another early chapter was the crusade by the Wobblies, the Industrial Workers of the World, to establish their right to free speech on the street corners. It was a pre–World War I equivalent of our fights today to establish the right to petition in shopping malls and to defend our right to sell our newspapers on street corners and at plant gates.

Our heritage also includes the fight against the arrest, trial, and imprisonment of Eugene Debs and other antidraft and anti-war fighters in World War I. It includes the fight against the anticommunist and anti-immigrant witch-hunt and deportations after that war, known as the Palmer raids (named after A. Mitchell Palmer, the attorney general at the time). It includes the fight against the monstrous frame-up and murder of Sacco and Vanzetti, and countless other cases of political persecution aimed at the working-class movement. It is a continuation of the fight waged on behalf of Julius and Ethel Rosenberg, who were martyrs of the witch-hunt in the 1950s.

Preparing for World War II

The secret police apparatus as we know it today began to take shape at the end of the 1930s, on the eve of the war. This is when our case begins.

Roosevelt was replacing the New Deal with the War Deal, as the imperialists prepared to subject humanity to the second world slaughter. As the U.S. capitalists got ready for war against their rivals abroad, they also prepared their offensive against the working class and against Blacks and Chicanos at home. Their aims were to silence all opponents of the war drive, to channel all motion toward a labor party back into the two capitalist parties, and to make working people accept the necessity of sacrifice. All struggles for improvements in wages and working conditions, or for an end to racial discrimination and segregation, had to be subordinated to the needs of the imperialist war.

Because they knew there would be opposition to this course, the employers decided on a big expansion of the FBI. Before this period the FBI was not primarily a political police force. For five years or so after World War I it had assumed this function. But by the mid-twenties, after widespread protests over FBI actions and with the decline of the labor radicalization, the capitalist government decided against a federal secret police agency. They relied instead on city and state cops, who had set up "bomb squads" and "radical divisions," and who had intimate connections with the network of private detective agencies.

These private cop operations had already acquired considerable experience in organizing spies and provocateurs against the labor movement, Black groups, and radical organizations. Moreover, they were less restricted than the federal government in the crimes they could commit with impunity.

The FBI is unleashed

But with the rise of the CIO and the deepgoing labor radicalization, the rulers knew that their war drive would require this whole operation to be centralized, upgraded, and brought directly under federal government control. In September 1936, J. Edgar Hoover, head of the FBI, acting under instructions from President Franklin Roosevelt, informed all FBI offices that "the Bureau desires to obtain from all possible sources information concerning subversive activities being conducted in the United States by Communists, Fascists, and representatives or advocates of other organizations advocating the overthrow or replacement of the Government of the United States by illegal methods."

By 1938, the Foreign Agents Registration Act was passed and Congress set up the Special Committee on Un-American Propaganda Activities (chaired by Texas Congressman Martin Dies), forerunner of the House Committee on Un-American Activities. The thought-control Smith Act and the Voorhis Act (which penalized political parties affiliated to international organizations) would be adopted in 1940. On September 6, 1939, Roosevelt issued a public statement instructing "all police officers, sheriffs, and other law enforcement officers in the United States promptly to turn over to the nearest representative of the Federal Bureau of Investigation any information obtained by them relating to espionage, counterespionage, sabotage, subversive activities and violations of the neutrality laws." The FBI established a General Intelligence Division in Washington, hired more agents, and began expanding its political informer network. The next year, FBI field offices were instructed to recruit or place informers in each of the nation's "war plants." By 1942, 23,476 federal finks were reporting on labor and radical activities in 4,000 factories and mills.

Although we didn't then know the secret moves that were being made to expand the FBI, working people saw the results immediately. In the Teamsters union in Minneapolis and throughout the central states region, union militants began to be framed up, arrested, and convicted. In each case, the prosecutors relied on testimony from informers and agents provocateurs. In his books *Teamster Politics* and *Teamster Bureaucracy* Farrell Dobbs records the direct intervention by the FBI, beginning with the 1939 frame-up of Teamster leaders in Omaha, Nebraska, and Des Moines and Sioux City, Iowa.

This antilabor police offensive culminated in the 1941 Smith Act trial in Minneapolis, in which eighteen leaders of the Teamsters union and of the Socialist Workers Party were convicted and imprisoned for advocating forbidden ideas—the things we advocate today. In that trial, the government had three objectives:

First, to purge the labor movement of rebels who wouldn't buy Roosevelt's war drive and militarization, and who were campaigning against it.

Second, to wipe out the stronghold of union democracy represented by the Minneapolis Teamsters, whose leadership was spreading class-struggle methods throughout the Midwest and educating workers in the need for political independence.

Third, to drive the Socialist Workers Party underground, to make it impossible for our party to function openly, to make us give up our public existence and accept illegality.

Although with the outbreak of the war the capitalists were able to achieve a good measure of success on the first two, they totally failed in their third objective.

The large-scale entry of the FBI into the political arena began around 1938, the same year our party was founded. They have been harassing us ever since. All we can say in our defense is that we have been harassing them for an equal period of time—and now, finally, we are getting the better of it.

After the Smith Act convictions all of this continued. During the war, the *Militant* was banned for a time from the mail. After the war came the antilabor, anticommunist witch-hunt, beginning with the establishment by the Truman administration of the attorney general's list of "subversive" organizations, an official government blacklist. Our party appeared on it from the beginning. We saw the long, vindictive government effort to victimize Jimmy Kutcher, a legless veteran of World War II who courageously insisted on his right to be a member of the SWP without losing his job or his veterans' benefits. Passports were denied to SWP leaders in an attempt to disrupt not only our party but the Fourth International, by preventing us from presenting our point of view at meetings of the International. Our members were witch-hunted out of the maritime industry, and many workers who were members or supporters of the party in other industries were fired.

In the early 1960s three YSA members were indicted for sedition in Bloomington, Indiana. In 1969 several of our members and other GIs were arrested for antiwar organizing at Fort Jackson, South Carolina. It took a nationwide defense campaign to free the Fort Jackson Eight. One of those young GIs, who became an undying foe of the political police, was Andrew Pulley, the SWP's 1980 presidential candidate.

These political police operations have continued right down to today with the Immigration Service's attempt to deport Héctor Marroquín—a move which we say, with total confidence, will not succeed!

Watergate and capitalist democracy

All of this brings us to 1973, when our suit against the FBI was finally filed, a century and a quarter after the fight got underway. Sometimes it's easy to forget how far we have come in the seven years since we first took the FBI to court, and how much we and others who have fought alongside us have accomplished.

In 1973 many of the crimes of the FBI were still secrets. We did not know in 1973 that the FBI was routinely—just about on a weekly schedule—burglarizing the headquarters of the party and homes of SWP members. We suspected they might be doing something like that, but we didn't know it. And of course, we had no evidence. We had no proof. We had never heard the term *mail cover,* nor had we any idea what it consisted of or how it worked. We had no indication that the FBI tape recorded all of our conventions. I, for one, never even suspected they systematically pawed through our garbage cans, in what we now know is termed a *trash cover.*

No one outside of the government had ever heard of the FBI conspiracy called the "SWP Disruption Program," or any of the other Cointelpro operations. No one knew how much the FBI had hounded Martin Luther King; that they had vowed to eliminate Malcolm X; that they had waged a war of disruption, infiltration, and frame-up against the American Indian Movement and the Black Panther Party; that they had targeted the women's movement for disruption; that they had used their agents provocateurs to disrupt the Communist Party by planting evidence smearing loyal CP members as agents—a technique known in the FBI as "putting the snitch jacket on."

No one knew then that the FBI had been intimately involved in the preparation for the murderous police raid on the Black Panthers in Chicago in 1969, when the cops emptied their guns into the body of Fred Hampton as he lay sleeping in his bed.

None of that was known back in 1973. That was the height of Watergate. Every day the newspapers were full of revelations about the outrageous acts and criminal deeds of Nixon and the White House "plumbers" against the Democratic Party, liberal groups, and critics of Nixon's Vietnam War strategy. The Watergate crimes were presented to the American people by the capitalist press and politicians as a terrible aberration caused by an evil and unbalanced Richard Nixon.

We had the TV spectacle of the congressional Watergate hearings, where the bipartisan orgy of hypocrisy broke all previous records. The Democrats and Republicans joined hands in "rescuing the Constitution" from the would-be tyrant Nixon. In reality they were engineering the real Watergate cover-up: the pretense that normal capitalist government functioning has nothing in common with the methods of the Nixon gang.

The labor bureaucrats tagged along, echoing the refrain that workers' rights would be secure if only Nixon were removed. The Communist Party and the entire petty-bourgeois left also accepted the framework presented by the ruling class. With more radical-sounding verbiage, they threw themselves into the debate over whether Nixon should be forced to resign or be impeached. Some of the more impressionable even went so far as to confuse bringing down Nixon with bringing down the government.

Class perspective

Our response was the opposite. We rejected the notion that Nixon alone was the problem. We said Watergate-style crimes show the evolution of the institutions of capitalist rule and the two capitalist parties. We said that the decisive question is how to advance the labor movement, the Black movement, the Chicano and Puerto Rican movements, along the road toward working-class political action independent of the Democratic and Republican parties. That is the only kind of political action that can defend democratic rights against the capitalist government and its police agencies.

Our lawsuit and the campaign we launched to win support for it were part of this class perspective. They were designed to dramatize the truth of what we were saying by forcing out before the American people some of the truth about the secret police. Our suit was also an example of how to take advantage of the contradictions that occur under bourgeois democracy and use them to defend and expand democratic rights.

In launching our educational campaign around this case we stressed a number of points. First, we said that the measures used by Nixon's plumbers—bugging, break-ins, frame-ups, and other "dirty tricks," were based on the methods the FBI and CIA have been using all along.

Second, we pointed out that their main enemy is not liberal groups like the Americans for Democratic Action or the American Civil Liberties Union—although they become victims of these methods too. The main target of the secret police is the working-class movement—the unions, the organizations of the oppressed nationalities, and socialist groups, including the SWP and the YSA.

Third, we insisted that there is a close connection between the methods and aims of U.S. imperialism abroad and its methods and aims against opponents of imperialism and of capitalism at home. You can't have a government that carries out a foreign policy that tramples on human rights and human values, commits unspeakable acts of violence and even genocide, overturns elected governments, subverts democracy—you can't have a government that does all that abroad and doesn't do essentially the same thing at home.

The methods revealed by Watergate were not an aberration, we argued. Watergate merely lifted a corner of the democratic mask concealing the true face of capitalist rule. That was what had been exposed. The use of secret police, informers, agents provocateurs, frame-ups, disruption efforts, and all the other things, are not incidental to capitalist rule. They are not secondary, not optional. They are permanent, basic, and essential.

This does not depend on the form of the capitalist state or the type of regime. We often say in popular explanations that the FBI uses police-state methods. This is true, of course. But the FBI methods are also the necessary methods of the political police under a bourgeois democracy. Think about this—the United States is not under fascist rule. It is not a police state. It is a bourgeois democracy. Among the most democratic of capitalist regimes anywhere in the world. Yet we have here this massive undercover repressive machine, an army of secret political police.

This undemocratic, repressive mechanism is part of the real content of capitalist democracy. That is why the workers' movement must constantly fight for its rights against this mechanism, fight to uncover it and get out the truth about it.

Marx explained over and over again the difference between the democratic forms and the real content of democracy under capitalism. Bourgeois democracy, like the capitalist economy, is built on formal equality between workers and capitalists. You are free to be exploited and the capitalist is equally free to exploit you. You and Rockefeller have equal rights to go to the free market and sell what you possess in order to make your fortune. You each have the same right to sell the commodities you possess. You have only your labor power; Rockefeller has "his" oil, "his" coal, and a few other things that he has acquired from your unpaid labor.

The same inequality in content exists in the protection of basic rights such as free speech, free press, freedom of association, equality of opportunity, and the right to privacy. These rights are, in form, guaranteed to everyone under the Constitution.

Free elections exist—for the Democrats and Republicans; workers' parties often can't get on the ballot.

Free press is guaranteed—to the owners of the capitalist media; others can't afford the price to make their views known to tens of millions.

Freedom of association is guaranteed—but for the working class it is only to the extent that the labor movement fights for and wins the right to assemble and to organize unions and political parties.

Equality of opportunity exists—for those with money, education, and training. For Blacks and Latinos, for women, equality of opportunity is a hoax.

The right to privacy is guaranteed—to the capitalists. Their financial records, true earnings, real holdings, and speed-up plans are shielded from public examination by laws protecting business secrets and corporate records. But the workers know no privacy from the bosses and their government, who amass files on our personal lives, our jobs and incomes, our political activities, even our opinions.

Beneath the forms of freedom and equality, the reality is that under capitalism all the social, economic, and political questions are decided by a tiny minority, with total contempt and disregard for the rights and needs of the great majority.

1973: 'It's better to be plaintiffs'

Our decision to proceed was based on sizing up the shift that was occurring in the relationship of class forces on a world scale, and the long-term tactical problems and divisions that this would keep producing for the capitalist class. The move we were making in 1973 could not have been made with success twenty, ten, or even five years earlier. We had to go through the Vietnam War, the end of the long economic expansion, and Watergate and all that went with it, before we could consider doing what we have done.

What was involved was a small party of revolutionary Marxists going up politically and legally against the secret police. Taking them on directly and aggressively. We know that a small group, with the right ideas, with the right degree of self-confidence, and with the right timing, can have a huge impact. A small organization acting in a bold way in the interests of an entire class can set an example and inspire broader forces to move. We decided that this was a good time to go after the FBI. And everything we said then is more true now.

In taking this initiative, we had to reject two arguments. The first was that by taking on the secret police we might provoke them into going after us. It would be like waving a red flag at the bull. The answer to that is we are always waving a red flag at the bull. And if the bull isn't coming after us in every way it can get away with at the moment, we're not doing something right, because that is the nature of us and that is the nature of the bull.

Second, a question was raised by some critics of the Socialist Workers Party as well as a few friends. Won't this initiative just promote illusions in the bourgeois courts? Can a revolutionary Marxist party really utilize the courts to advance our aims?

The answer to that is there is nothing new about using the bourgeois courts. Marxists have been in and out of courts ever since 1848. The working-class movement long ago rejected the approach of the syndicalists, such as the IWW, of turning your back on the judge and the court, refusing to put up a defense because you reject the authority of the capitalist courts. This is the approach being used today, for example, by the alleged members of the Puerto Rican FALN indicted in Chicago. These are people we admire for their courage and for their dedication to a cause we support, but not for their courtroom strategy. They deny themselves the opportunity to use the courtroom to take advantage of some of the contradictions between the letter and reality of justice under capitalism and, most importantly, as a forum from which to reach working people with their ideas and explain the justice of their cause. We reject this ultraleft approach.

Some of the best and most effective propaganda has been made by revolutionary fighters from the prisoner's dock. Marx, Wilhelm Liebknecht, Leon Trotsky, Rosa Luxemburg, James P. Cannon, and Fidel Castro are among the examples.

What we saw was an opportunity to fight for our rights in court not as defendants but as prosecutors of the FBI and CIA and the whole rotten gang. And we can now say, to paraphrase the actress Mae West: we have been defendants and we have been plaintiffs, and all in all, being plaintiffs is better.

So we proceeded. We had the good fortune to have as our chief attorney Leonard B. Boudin, without question the most able and dedicated Bill of Rights attorney in the country, who has been the general counsel for the Socialist Workers Party and Young Socialist Alliance for many years.

We sat down with our legal staff and drew up what lawyers call a complaint, in which you outline your case. In the complaint, we charged that the government, the FBI, and other secret police agencies have been involved in a conspiracy since 1938 to disrupt the SWP. (Remember, we had never heard of the "SWP Disruption Program" at that time.) We charged that this conspiracy involved the use of informers, burglaries, blacklists, wiretaps, bugs, mail openings, and other illegal acts. We charged that the cops collaborated with right-wing terrorists in physical attacks against the party and the YSA. We put into this complaint everything that we could think of, everything that the history of the workers' movement since 1848 shows that the secret police do.

We filed the suit on July 18, 1973. At first it didn't make a big splash. It seemed to most people to be peripheral to the exposés about Nixon's gang. It took some time before people saw that the lurid activities of the plumbers were peripheral to the illegal war against us and others that has been waged for decades by the entire non-plumber, "legitimate," secret police apparatus.

But we now know that inside the government, in the Justice Department, at the FBI, inside the White House, our complaint hit like a bombshell. Because as it turns out, *it was all true.* Exactly, precisely, true. Every "wild accusation" that we put in the complaint hit home.

A new conspiracy

The government's response, we now know, was to set in motion an entire new conspiracy. A conspiracy to cover up the truth. Coordinated moves were undertaken to counter the suit. Government officials lied repeatedly in court. They plotted to obstruct the suit, to defy court orders, to disguise even the documents that they had to turn over, to censor out the relevant parts.

Politically, they were trying desperately to confine the revelations to the Nixon White House. "Nixon's the one," they said. Get rid of Nixon and everything will be fine. But by the time they got rid of Nixon, they couldn't contain it. There was too much: too many crimes, too widespread distrust of the methods and objectives of the government, of the institutions of capitalist rule. The American people had gone through the lies about Vietnam, they had lived through the police brutalization of the minority communities, they knew about the lies and continual coverups about Watergate.

Under this pressure, deepgoing tactical divisions persisted within the ruling class. And as a result the stories about the real crimes of the CIA and the FBI began to come out. The tales about Nixon's plumbers paled in comparison. Assassinations, reactionary coups all over the world, "destabilization" operations, payoffs and bribes to corrupt politicians and bloody dictators on five continents. And similar methods in this country. This had to follow. If you conspire to assassinate Fidel Castro and sabotage the Cuban revolution, you're going to do whatever you can get away with to the defenders of the Cuban revolution in this country. It makes total sense that the same people would conspire to assassinate Malcolm X. Massive disruption programs, blanket surveillance, wholesale violations of the Bill of Rights. It all began to emerge.

It would be a foolish exaggeration to say that our suit *caused* this to happen. Broader forces, including the deep public loss of confidence in the truthfulness of the capitalist government, were responsible for it. But it would be equally foolish to underestimate the central role that our initiative played in forcing all this to light. Because of the timing, because of the aggressive ways we pursued it, because we were so right about the charges and had the goods on the FBI, because we correctly judged the scope of the shift in the world relationship of class forces against the American exploiters and the resulting tactical divisions and disorientation, we played a central role all the way through this.

One of our main contributions was inspiring other victims,

especially leaders of the Black movement, to do the same thing, to fight back against the FBI. We also charted important new constitutional ground, in a case that has already gone three times to the court of appeals and twice to the Supreme Court—before even coming to trial.

The ruling class faced a tough problem. The FBI and the CIA were becoming discredited. Millions of people no longer believed that they told the truth or that they were in the business of defending democracy. This was a problem because the capitalist class *must have* an effective political police force. They had to find a way to strengthen the FBI and the CIA, to refurbish them, to make them operational once again.

So they decided, just as they had been compelled to do at a certain point with Nixon, to cut their losses. They opted for letting some of the truth come out, so as to be able to cut short the disclosures, reverse the process, contain it, and put the secret police back into fighting condition. They decided it was necessary to temporarily "vent" the FBI and the CIA. And that's when the big revelations took place in 1975 and 1976.

Sensational congressional hearings were held. There were revelations in the press day after day. And a substantial part of this involved our party. Revelations in our case got big coverage. We were on national network news a number of times. The courtroom where our suit was being heard in New York became an arena in which at least part of the truth was laid before the American people. The SWP and YSA became known throughout the country, to millions, as organizations that know how to fight, that understand the importance of democratic rights, and that are not afraid to take on the FBI. This added up to a historic gain for our movement in this country.

One of the obstacles the ruling class had to overcome was resistance inside the ranks of the FBI itself to this new course. Some FBI agents refused to quietly take the rap for the crimes. "We were just carrying out the assignments you gave us," they said. And a little more of the truth came out this way. Sometimes the rulers even had to play a little rough with the FBI, in order to be able to turn it into the kind of political police force they need for the 1980s.

Just like attack dogs, these FBI agents trained in the 1940s, '50s, and '60s didn't respond well to unaccustomed commands to heel. Many couldn't restrain themselves. They kept talking like it was still the 1950s. So there was a bit of housecleaning, and it wasn't all amicable. In fact some of it was literally bloody.

Of course, the capitalist politicians and news media presented all of these revelations with their own twist. It's all in the past, they said. It's all over. Finished. Nixon's gone. J. Edgar Hoover is safely in his grave. The turbulent times of the 1960s are behind us.

New cover-ups

Then, in the autumn of 1976, came a new turning point. The attorney general publicly announced that he was directing the FBI to terminate its investigation of our movement after nearly forty years. This is part of the new cover-up, a lie built on top of other lies. They never ended the investigation. They shuffled some papers and relabeled some files. They made some tactical retreats. We made them back off a little, but only temporarily. And the FBI certainly doesn't think we are less of a threat to them than before.

After this announcement, all of a sudden, there was an end to the publicity about our case. Newspaper, television, and wire service reporters all told us that word had come down from their editors, "no more big play to the SWP case." And, like magic, the revelations on the FBI and CIA crimes were no longer topics of interest to the big news media. That's the "free press" in action.

We were able to break through the news blackout on more than one occasion because such important things kept happening. Especially the contempt-of-court citation against Attorney General Griffin Bell for defying a court order to hand over to our attorneys a representative sample of eighteen informer files. But even then there was no editorial outcry about how bad it was that the nation's top law-enforcement officer was openly defying the court. None pointed out that Bell's challenge to the Constitution was more serious than any move Nixon ever made. Nixon never openly refused to comply with a court order.

Instead there were editorials in the capitalist press explaining the need for an "informer privilege." We really must have informers, to use against the drug pushers, the Mafia, and foreign agents, they argued. Bell was painted as courageous for defying the law for this sacred principle. He was willing to risk jail for his beliefs, they said. He was even compared to Martin Luther King!

And, of course, Bell was eventually upheld by the court of appeals and the Supreme Court. The judges based their ruling on a novel but simple legal doctrine: the attorney general is above the law! Another lesson in bourgeois equality before the law.

Role of liberals

In this campaign to restore faith in the FBI and CIA, to make them stronger and more effective, to convince people that the crimes are over, a crucial role was assigned to the liberals. This was easier because after 1976 the Carter administration, a Democratic Party administration, was in office. The Carter Justice Department went to work to get the liberal American Civil Liberties Union, and others who speak in the name of civil liberties, to cooperate in this process. They all agreed that new "restraints" must be put on the FBI and CIA. They eagerly allowed themselves to be roped into drafting legislative "charters" for the FBI and CIA—giving them legal cover for their criminal activities.

They came up with new controls on wiretapping, for instance. The liberals said, "Wiretapping is bad. But sometimes you do need wiretapping because you have organized crime and foreign agents and drug smugglers," and so on and so forth. So they agreed on a reform: no wiretapping without a court-approved warrant. Then they said, "But you can't expect every judge to understand all these sensitive cases, so we'll set up a special court to issue the wiretap warrants. And, of course, this court can't be public, because people being wiretapped would know about it, so we'll do it in secret. We'll have a secret court."

And they set one up.

There is today a secret federal wiretap court. You can't find out who's on it. You can't find out where it is. You can't find out when the government comes to make a request for wiretaps. It is called the Foreign Intelligence Surveillance Court. The only thing we know is that this court has never turned down a government request for a wiretap! This is a great liberal reform. If we continue like this we may get a special informer court, to issue warrants for informers. Maybe we'll even get a special "black bag job" court, to issue warrants for FBI burglaries. Then maybe the CIA will get a special court to authorize assassinations.

Another side of this new relationship between the FBI and the liberals was being worked out more or less behind the scenes. This involved the outcome of many of the lawsuits that had been filed, almost all of them after we filed ours. The success we had and the revelations about FBI crimes led to a number of suits, many of which were modeled on ours.

After the so-called end to the investigation and the proclamation of new "guidelines" for the FBI in 1976, and after the Carter administration took office, these suits began to be settled out of court. We were not totally surprised by this. The government had also approached us to negotiate a settlement of our suit. We pursued this because if we can settle the case to our advantage, we want to do it. There is no political principle involved. If we can get a favorable ruling, it makes no difference whether it comes from a judge after a trial or from an agreement with the attorney general before a trial.

When we pursued the negotiations with the Department of Justice, however, we found that they weren't really offering anything. If we would drop the suit, they would settle the case for a token amount of money and make a solemn statement that from now on they would abide by the law. But they have to say they abide by the law anyway. So this did not strike us as much of a concession.

Blessing the 'new FBI'

As it turned out, others had different reactions. A large number of out-of-court settlements have been arranged. By and large they add up to part of the cover-up.

The first tentative step in establishing this pattern was a settlement reached in December 1975 in a suit brought by the American Friends Service Committee and Philadelphia Resistance, pacifist groups that had been targeted by the FBI. The agreement includes provisions like this:

The FBI will not "subject the individual plaintiffs to photographic or physical surveillance *without reasonable cause . . .*"; "subject the individual plaintiffs to electronic surveillance except as specifically permitted by court order *or under circumstances where such surveillance is permitted without court order under the Fourth Amendment [!]*"; or "enter the homes or offices of the plaintiffs or limit their freedom of movement without a warrant . . . *unless such warrantless action is preceded by the existence of sufficient evidence that will support a warrantless entry or limitation of freedom in accordance with the provisions and application of the Fourth Amendment of the Constitution of the United States*" (my emphasis).

The plaintiffs were paid $1,600 for their costs in filing the suit, and dropped all their claims.

Maybe there are circumstances here we don't know about. Maybe the case was very weak; maybe the AFSC and the Resistance group couldn't afford financially to sustain it; or maybe some other factors were involved. But the settlement itself, agreed to by the plaintiffs, is nothing less than a license for the FBI to do all it has been doing—only now with the victims' apparent consent.

More recently, in April 1979, Jane Fonda reached an agreement with the FBI to settle her case. The FBI had sought to disrupt her career and defame her because Fonda uncompromisingly spoke out against the Vietnam War and took some explicitly radical positions. The Fonda settlement is based on the "FBI Guidelines," which were put into effect in 1976. These guidelines are supposed to define narrower grounds for deciding whom the FBI can "investigate," and contain mechanisms for periodic review—by the FBI and the attorney general!—of the FBI's disruptive and spy techniques. As you might expect, the drift of the guidelines is that, from now on, the FBI will obey the law.

The settlement of the Fonda case states that these guidelines "would have precluded the Domestic Security Investigation of plaintiff *in the form in which it was conducted*" (my emphasis). It goes on to list the following "points of understanding":

"1. The Federal Bureau of Investigation is not now conducting and will not in the future conduct a Domestic Security Investigation of plaintiff *except as may be permitted* by the Attorney-General's Guidelines for Domestic Security Investigations, effective April 5, 1976 and as they may be modified by Act of Congress or the Attorney General.

"2. Domestic Security Investigations as described in Paragraph 1 above will not employ any technique designed to impair the lawful and constitutionally protected political conduct of plaintiff or to defame her character or reputation. . . .

"4. Electronic surveillance of the oral or wire communications of plaintiff in the course of any Domestic Security Investigation shall be conducted in accordance with applicable Supreme Court law . . . and applicable Acts of the Congress . . ." (my emphasis).

Fonda and her ACLU lawyers agreed to drop the suit without any payment of damages, and to waive any and all claims she might have had for anything the FBI did to her. Often under capitalism, of course, you have to settle for less than what you are entitled to. The settlement in the Fonda case, however, is quite a bad one from the standpoint of the enemies of the FBI. It is a disservice that is all the harder to accept because it is inconceivable that Fonda and the ACLU had to throw in the towel because of a lack of financial resources. It is more likely that Fonda, a liberal and a Democrat, really does have confidence in the "new FBI," believes it has a legitimate role, and wanted to do her part to add to its authority.

Chicago suit

By far the worst settlement from our standpoint, is one that has not yet been signed, but is now being negotiated, in the *ACLU v. Chicago* case. We are obligated not to keep silent while these negotiations are under way because this is a case in which we are among the plaintiffs. This suit (actually two suits that have been consolidated) was filed by many organizations in Chicago that were victimized by the vast campaign of terror, abuse, spying, and disruption waged by the FBI, the Chicago cops, Military Intelligence, the ultraright Legion of Justice, and other cop forces.

Among other things, this campaign included numerous terrorist attacks carried out by the Legion of Justice goons, with active cooperation from the Chicago cops and political police. The 113th Military Intelligence Group, based at Evanston, Illinois, provided the legion with mace, tear gas, electronic surveillance equipment, and money. Chicago cops provided protection for the raids and burglaries. In return, the legionnaires turned over to the cops and the army the files, records, and books they seized in the raids.

In November 1969 our headquarters in Chicago was invaded by legion members armed with clubs and mace. Several of our members were injured. Another raid targeted an apartment that was the YSA headquarters in DeKalb, Illinois. Men wearing ski masks and armed with tire irons and mace attacked the YSA members, beating them and macing them. One of the potentially most deadly attacks took place two days after the brutal assassination of Black Panther leaders Fred Hampton and Mark Clark. On December 6, 1969, some thirty cops, some with guns drawn, stormed into the Chicago SWP and YSA headquarters, claiming they had received "anonymous tips" that a shoot-out was in progress. Fortunately, they could find no pretext to open fire. Others were victims of similar police tactics in this period.

Now a settlement of the combined suit is being cooked up by the ACLU and the Justice Department. From the draft we have seen, this is shaping up into an unconscionable betrayal. Not only does this proposed settlement contain the usual empty assertions, but it goes further. It contains language whose only purpose is to lend political credence to the FBI's new image, thus opening the way to deepening abuses and attacks.

Here are a few of the key passages:

"With respect to the FBI, the Attorney General's Guidelines governing Domestic Security Investigations became effective approximately six months after plaintiffs' first Complaint against the federal defendants was filed. Initially, and for several years, plaintiffs were deeply concerned by ambiguities and omissions in these Guidelines, and by serious questions as to how they would be interpreted and implemented, and indeed as to whether they would remain in effect at all. Plaintiffs had similar concerns relating to the other Guidelines and procedures promulgated by the federal defendants after the Complaint was filed.

"However, plaintiffs' extensive discovery concerning the interpretations of the Guidelines by the Department of Justice and the FBI during the four years since their promulgation has persuaded plaintiffs that the Guidelines and other post-filing laws and procedures governing the FBI afford a reasonable basis upon which to settle this litigation. In arriving at this conclusion, plaintiffs take particular note of the following:

"(1) Both in the Chicago area and nationwide, there has been a dramatic reduction in the number of FBI domestic security investigations since the Guidelines were promulgated. . . .

"(2) This significant reduction in the number of domestic security investigations reflects in large part the manner in which the Attorney General, his Office of Intelligence Policy and Review (formerly the Investigation Review Unit), and the FBI have interpreted and implemented the Guidelines for Domestic Security Investigations.

"The Attorney General initiated the implementation of the Guidelines by disapproving ten of the first nineteen full domestic security investigations of organizations upon which he made a determination. Among the domestic security investigations he discontinued were those of the Socialist Workers Party and the Communist Party, U.S.A. . . . [Referring to the CP, a footnote here adds: "However, the investigation of the Communist Party, U.S.A., was converted to one conducted pursuant to the Attorney General's Guidelines governing foreign counterintelligence investigations." What a comfort!]

"(3) Even though most domestic security investigations were thus 'closed' under the Guidelines, plaintiffs were nonetheless deeply troubled by the FBI's practice—which continued in the Chicago Field Office until at least mid-1977—of routinely disseminating informants' reports to 'closed' or 'dead' domestic security files on persons named in the reports, and/or indexing such persons to the reports. The result of this practice was that the FBI continued to amass domestic security files and index cards on persons who could not be 'investigated' under the Guidelines. Plaintiffs discovered a number of 'closed' and 'dead' domestic security files in the Chicago Field Office which, during 1976 and until mid-1977, continued to be expanded by the same kind of information (reports on political meetings and demonstrations) obtained by the same means (informants) as had been the case before these investigations and files were 'closed'. However, plaintiffs' discovery of FBI files indicates that these objectionable dissemination and indexing practices have been discontinued since late 1977. . . .

"(4) Plaintiffs' discovery indicates that the number of investigations under the Attorney General's Guidelines relating to Civil Disorders has been even smaller than the number of investigations under the Domestic Security Guidelines.

"(5) Plaintiffs' discovery also indicates that the FBI is conducting only a relatively small number of foreign counterintelligence investigations of domestic groups and individuals associated with them. The number of these investigations is somewhat larger than the number of domestic security investigations. These mainly [!] involve investigations of groups and individuals who are engaged in serious and violent acts of international terrorism, activities in preparation therefor [!], or who knowingly aid and abet persons engaged in international terrorism. [!] . . . Although some of the foreign counterintelligence investigations involve the Communist Party, U.S.A., and related groups and individuals, plaintiffs' discovery indicates that these investigations are not simply a relabeling and continuation of the 'domestic security' investigation of the Communist Party, U.S.A., which was terminated in late 1976."

This, of course, is a colossal lie. It amounts to making the victims co-conspirators in the cover-up. The ACLU and others are being drawn into this campaign to convince the American people that the "new FBI" deserves trust and confidence. We have formally notified all sides that we will not be party to this or any similar settlement.

By watching the role of the ACLU lawyers, you get a good lesson in the difference between liberals and principled civil libertarians. There are some supporters of capitalism—liberals and conservatives alike—who are consistent defenders of civil liberties, what we could call democrats with a small *d*. We have all met individuals of this kind, and we value their integrity and their principled stands. But they all suffer from terrible contradictions.

Those who support the Democratic or Republican parties support the deadliest enemy of democratic rights. Those whose allegiance is to the capitalist system support a system that can survive only by denying democratic rights to the oppressed and exploited. These contradictions are becoming more and more acute as the class polarization deepens and the rulers intensify their offensive against workers' standard of living and rights.

It's not just that liberals are "unreliable" allies of the workers in the fight for democratic rights today. The liberal defenders of American imperialism were the architects and engineers who—during and after World War II—built the entire worldwide machinery of spying and counterrevolution that became the CIA. It was the liberals who set up the original "loyalty" programs, blacklists, and other key building blocks of the witch-hunt that led, among other things, to the cold-blooded judicial murder of Julius and Ethel Rosenberg for the crime of being Communists and Jews.

The working class, with its most oppressed sectors—oppressed nationalities and women, is the social force with a real stake in defending democratic freedoms to the end. The liberals want various reforms—some that extend and some that restrict democratic rights—in order to preserve capitalism. The working class wants democratic rights protected and extended so that we can live without "Big Brother" spying on our political and personal lives, and so we can untie our hands to fight for our interests and to fight to bring a workers' government to power.

So in this area, too, we can rely on a variation of the slogan of the Nicaraguan revolutionary leader Augusto César Sandino: "Only the workers and farmers will go all the way"—in the fight for democratic rights. This is fundamentally why our party has been able to play such a prominent role, a role out of proportion to our size, in the fight against the FBI and CIA, while others with more resources have been inconsistent and hesitant.

Their settlement offer . . . and ours

Now I want to report to you the latest attempts by the government to get us to go along with this pattern of betrayals of the fight for democratic rights.

From time to time we have met with officials in the Department of Justice to discuss the possibility of an out-of-court settlement. We have thoroughly pursued this possibility, and will continue to do so. If the government would recognize in legally binding form our rights as a legal political party, and would agree to a reasonable payment in compensation for its past crimes, we would settle. Keeping this case alive is enormously expensive, and consumes considerable resources. A settlement would avoid the additional burdens of a trial and, inevitably, years of appeals before a final judgment would take effect. For all of these reasons, even though we may have to settle for less than we are entitled to, or would like to get, we have seriously pursued the concrete possibilities of a negotiated settlement.

At a meeting in July 1980, the Justice Department negotiators encouraged us to go along with the pattern of settlements I have just described. Everyone else is accepting this pattern, they said. We just don't understand why you won't go along. In stressing this, they were revealing a real problem they have. They really do need us to accept the settlement pattern. Because of the legal and political role of our case, because it is so well known, because of its sweeping character, we are a major obstacle to their whole plan. If we don't go along, the whole thing doesn't work, and may come apart.

We explained that this pattern of settlements was totally unacceptable to us. We made a counterproposal for them to consider. We submitted a draft of a settlement we could accept. It's a lengthy legal document, but it boils down to two points:

First, we want them to affirm in court that what we advocate, what we say, the ideas that we stand for, are legal and protected by the Bill of Rights. This includes our resolutions, our campaign platforms, the ideas that we promulgate.

Second, they must agree in court that what we *do* is legal—that is, putting the ideas into practice, here and abroad. Building a revolutionary party is an activity protected by the First Amendment. These two points, after all, are what this case has been about from the beginning.

There is no secret about either our ideas or our actions. The ideas we advocate are published and available for all to read and evaluate. As Marx and Engels said, we communists disdain to conceal our views. It's all up front. There are no secret plans or programs.

Our activities are no secret either, because the FBI has compiled a detailed record of everything we've done for forty years. We consider that to be a violation of our rights. But since they've done it, since the detailed written record of it exists, we propose to turn it around and use it to our advantage. We defy them to come up with a single act or statement in the forty-plus years in which the FBI has been spying on every meeting, every discussion, every demonstration and rally, and has bugged every gathering of the leadership of the SWP and the Fourth International. We defy them to produce evidence of a *single* act not fully protected by the Bill of Rights.

So we said, if the government will agree, in formal court papers, to the simple proposition that every person in this country has the democratic right to advocate the replacement of capitalism with socialism and to work to bring it about, and that they can't be prosecuted or harassed or "investigated" by the FBI because they exercise that right, then we will be happy to sit down and discuss how much money the government has to give us to compensate for their past violations.

We had one final meeting at the Justice Department in October 1980—just a few days before the election. Their position hadn't changed, and neither had ours. But they offered one new argument: if you don't accept our offer, these liberals told us, and if Carter loses the election, then you will be faced with a much tougher proposal from Reagan.

They were disappointed when we didn't fall for this "lesser evil" argument. But they had nothing more to say. So we left, telling them they had better start getting their case ready for the trial.

An agent exposed
Now, I want to report one of the most important victories we won in 1980.

As we have already reported to the party branches and all members, Edward Heisler informed us by letter in June that he has been a paid informer for the FBI. According to his story he became an informer in 1966 and ceased being an informer in 1971. All indications are, however, that Heisler was an agent when he joined our movement in 1960 and that he continued his disruptive activities right up until the day he acted, for reasons still unknown to us, to reveal his cop role to the party.

Edward Heisler joined the YSA in Milwaukee in 1960. He came from a working-class family. He first came to our attention when he started publicly challenging and debating an ultra-right-wing outfit he had been drawn around. He moved to Chicago in the early 1960s, where he stayed for more than a decade.

In Chicago, Heisler went to work on the railroad. As a member of the United Transportation Union there, he played a prominent role in the movement that developed among rail workers between 1969 and 1971 to win the right of the membership to vote on union contracts. The UTU Right to Vote Committee, of which Heisler served as secretary, won active support from thousands of rail workers, and received the endorsement of hundreds of UTU locals in the United States and Canada. At the 1971 UTU convention, delegates supporting the right to vote on contracts came within a hair's breadth of getting a majority.

In 1974 he was the party's candidate for U.S. Senate from Illinois. At the SWP convention in 1975 he was elected an alternate member of the National Committee. In 1977 he was elected a regular member of the National Committee, and reelected again in 1979, our last convention.

In 1975 Heisler moved to New York and worked on the staff of the party's 1976 presidential campaign committee. During 1977 he worked out of the SWP national office as a member of the national trade union coordinating committee of the party.

At the end of 1977 he was assigned by the party to go back into industry. He moved to Chicago. Heisler requested and we agreed that he was to have no assignments and no contact with the Chicago branch because he said he feared he had been black-listed on the railroad and wanted to maximize his chance of getting hired. He reported that he was unable to get a job on the railroad. After about a year, he moved to Los Angeles, where he also failed to get back on the railroad. In Los Angeles for the past year and a half, under the guise of one medical problem after another, he has been relatively inactive.

What are the lessons of this experience for the party? These lessons aren't fundamentally new. The working-class movement, and the communist wing of the workers' movement in particular, has faced finks and provocateurs since 1848. We have been through this before. Marx and Engels wrote about the police agents' dirty work, and explained in depth what type of people they are, how they are hooked. Marx described the anti-working-class, lumpen, and bohemian attitudes they develop and milieus they are attracted to, and the forms of their corruption. (See *Collected Works,* Marx and Engels, Progress Publishers, 1978, vol. 10, pp. 311–25; and *The Cologne Communist Trial,* Karl Marx, International Publishers, 1971.) They haven't changed. Not a bit.

The first and most immediate lesson concerns our policy prohibiting the use of marijuana and all other illegal drugs by our members. The purpose of this policy is to make victimizations and frame-ups more difficult for the cops to pull off against our members. We don't yet know all of the provocative and disruptive activities Heisler was carrying out. But we have learned that he waged a campaign, until the day we expelled him, to undermine this policy. He worked at this energetically, persistently, with vim and vigor.

We have learned a lot about Heisler since the party expelled him, from our members and from friends not in the party. What we know so far points to a major disruption effort by the FBI around the marijuana question.

Heisler selectively talked to SWP and YSA members trying to convince them that our policy on illegal drugs isn't really what we say it is. He told them that some leaders of the party smoke pot, and that others know they do and wink at it. No names, of course, were ever given.

He privately argued that the prohibition on drug use and on socializing with others while they are using drugs cannot and should not be applied universally in the party. He insisted, for instance, that "valuable trade union comrades" should not be thrown out of the party for violating discipline on this. He argued, in private, when given the slightest encouragement, that the policy itself was not necessary, that it was the result of over-cautious and rigid thinking. He said most workers smoke dope, so what's the big deal?

The more we learn about Heisler's actions as an agent provocateur in our ranks, the more it becomes clear that promoting a breakdown in our policy against use by party members of illegal drugs was his major disruption angle. Why? Because he was not able to act as a provocateur on other political questions.

So far as we know, he never came up to some member, privately, and argued that our position against individual terrorism was too "rigid." He never said, "Hey, why don't you and I toss a few molotov cocktails at the army recruiting station on the way home tonight?" He never said, "Say, why don't we get together sometime and cast a vote for some liberal Democrat? Lots of people in the plants do it. Hey, it feels good. . . ." He would have been nailed in an instant. So he worked the dope front.

Heisler did us some damage, to the extent he was able to confuse a small number of members about our policy on drugs. But the outcome has greatly strengthened the party. The entire party is stronger now in understanding why our ban on use of illegal drugs is necessary and correct, and why it is and must be universally applied.

If you think about this whole experience, there is an apparent paradox that has to be explained. How is it that a traitor like Heisler was able to carry out useful party work, including in the mass movement and as a candidate and party spokesperson?

What about the UTU right-to-vote campaign, in which Heisler played a prominent role. How do we explain that? Was the Right to Vote Committee off the mark politically? No. Heisler helped organize a campaign, along the lines the party decided on, to strengthen the union. He carried out other campaigns of the party as well. The Right to Vote Committee wasn't the FBI's creation. It wasn't their line. The FBI is not for democratizing the unions. The strategy and tactics Heisler followed were the strategy and tactics of the party, worked out by the members we had in the UTU, the leadership of the Chicago party branch, and the Political Committee.

Heisler was bound by the program and discipline of the party in his political work. Mostly he was bound by the understanding by the membership of our political line. In order to stay in the party—to "earn" his pay as an informer—he had to, by and large, carry out in public the program of the party. He was hemmed in.

The Malinovsky case

This was all explained by the Bolshevik Party, and in particular by Lenin. They had plenty of experience with enemy agents in their ranks. The classic case involved a man by the name of Roman Malinovsky. Malinovsky was a worker, a member of the Bolshevik Party, and an agent in the service of the Okhrana. With Lenin's support he got elected to the Central Committee operating inside Russia, in the underground. And in 1912, when elections were held to the Duma, the parliament under the tsar, Lenin proposed that Malinovsky be among those nominated by the Bolsheviks. He was, said Lenin, a worker and a diligent member of the party. Malinovsky was nominated and elected. Later, after the revolution, when the Okhrana files were opened and the whole Malinovsky story was revealed, the Bolsheviks learned that the cops had been so anxious to have Malinovsky elected that they helped him out by arresting his opponents!

Malinovsky was elected head of the Bolshevik fraction in the Duma. As a result, he became a chief spokesperson for the Bolsheviks. The Duma fraction played a very important role in this period. The party itself was outlawed and had to function in illegal and semilegal ways. But the deputies to the Duma had a different legal standing. They were, to some degree, protected. They functioned openly. They had offices, something like congressional offices.

As a result, much of the organizational work of the party was carried out through the Duma members. Underground workers from all over Russia came to their offices. Money collected for the election campaigns was turned in. Subscribers to *Pravda,* the party paper, were handed in to the fraction. Many of the arrangements for routine illegal functioning were handled in this way. And, of course, through Malinovsky, names were turned over to the cops. Untold numbers of Bolsheviks were victimized. Many were killed as a result of his treachery.

The speeches given by the Duma deputies could be published and legally distributed afterward. Malinovsky, as head of the fraction, gave many of the important speeches. But he was not able to say what he wanted. Lenin and Zinoviev, in exile, wrote out in advance many of the key speeches and they were smuggled into the country. At first, Malinovsky would take the text of the speech to the cops, and they would sit down and try to edit it. Soften this point, drop that point, reduce the effectiveness of the text. Then Malinovsky would bring the speech to the fraction, and say, "I think we should soften this point, drop that point," and so on. The fraction said, "No! You give the speech the party has prepared. That's our line." So he had to. He had no choice.

The political education and discipline of the fraction, and of the party in general, was such that this police agent couldn't divert it. He couldn't change the line. He was forced to move in step with the party and effectively promote the political positions of the party. The program of the party and the Leninist concept of revolutionary centralism meant that even an enemy agent in the strategic position Malinovsky attained was trapped. He was locked in a steel trap more powerful than the Okhrana—a Leninist party.

He did damage, but he couldn't alter the course of the party.

That course, as we know, led to a workers' and peasants' government before 1917 ended. After the February 1917 revolution, many of the informer files were uncovered, and the role of Malinovsky finally exposed. He had fled the country after a couple of years in the Duma. Rumors about Malinovsky had circulated widely for some time, and Lenin insisted, in the absence of any proof, on defending Malinovsky. He explained that rumors like those did more harm to the party than any agent provocateur. Lenin had denounced the Mensheviks and other enemies of the Bolsheviks who persisted in circulating these rumors.

Lenin drew the lessons of this experience after the truth about Malinovsky's employment by the Okhrana finally came out:

"It is obvious that by helping to elect an *agent-provocateur* to the Duma and by removing, for that purpose, all the competitors of the Bolshevik candidate, the secret police were guided by a vulgar conception of Bolshevism, or rather a distorted caricature of Bolshevism. They imagined that the Bolsheviks would 'arrange an armed insurrection.' In order to keep all the threads of this coming insurrection in their hands, they thought it worth while departing from their own standpoint and having Malinovsky elected both to the Duma and to our Central Committee.

"But when the police achieved both these aims they found that Malinovsky was transformed into a link of the long and solid chain connecting in various ways our legal base with the two chief organs by which the party influenced the *masses,* namely *Pravda* and the Duma fraction. The *agent-provocateur* had to protect both these organs in order to justify his vocation. . . .

"Malinovsky could and did ruin individuals, but he could neither hold back nor control the growth of the Party nor in any way affect the increase of its importance to the masses, its influence over hundreds of thousands of workers (through strikes, which increased after April 1912, etc.) . . ."

In explaining the cops' "distorted caricature of Bolshevism," Lenin was restating a point made by Marx and Engels. In an

1850 article dealing with police spies and conspiracies, they wrote: "A true revolution is the exact opposite of the ideas of a *mouchard* [police spy], who like the 'men of action' sees in every revolution the work of a small coterie" (Marx and Engels, *Collected Works,* vol. 10, p. 314).

Just consider what this episode reveals about the power of the Socialist Workers Party. Our party is so strong that even an enemy right in the midst of the party, in the national office, on the national committee, couldn't affect the political course of the party. We now know he caused us problems, but the problems were small compared to the overall work of the party. We used him; he was little able to use us.

The Heisler episode offers a gauge of where we are in constructing the kind of party we need. We measure up pretty well. The political homogeneity of the party, the discipline of the party, loyalty to the party comes only from one source: the understanding each and every member has of our program, and the confidence we have in that program, in our class, and in ourselves. That is where our strength lies. And that is the strength that Heisler and the FBI ran up against.

'Bag jobs' and dead bodies

A second victory we scored recently was forcing the government finally to cough up a document bearing the delicately worded title: "Summary of Inquiry Into the Nondisclosure of FBI Bag Jobs in the Socialist Workers Party Litigation."

The background to this is as follows: When we filed our suit in 1973, we charged that, among other things, the FBI had conspired to commit burglaries against our headquarters and the homes of our members. The government denied this charge in court, in sworn statements. They denied it repeatedly. However, in 1976, as a result of the process I described earlier, the FBI was forced to admit that yes, after all, there had been burglaries, known in FBI jargon as "black bag jobs." They had to admit that their previous denials were lies. At that time, Judge Griesa demanded to know who was responsible for the lies; he demanded an investigation. The results of this investigation were finally produced in court.

I hope we can publish this "Nondisclosure" document. It is an important part of the record of this entire period, and it has facts that have not come to light anywhere else.

It shows the extent to which our case sent shock waves throughout Washington when it was filed. It describes meetings in the White House over how they were going to respond to this. It shows some of the bureaucratic squabbles that reflected the ruling-class debate over how much to let come out. And it gives an indication of the role that our case played in blowing the lid off this whole thing.

In addition, it provides proof of deliberate and naked obstruction of justice on the part of the FBI.

It details, for example, how the government attorneys tried to harass us with demands for information about the SWP, in an attempt to make us limit the scope of the case. According to the report, the sole purpose of "several hundred questions . . . designed to explore the history and past ideology of the SWP . . . was to encourage the plaintiffs to agree to limit discovery to a relatively recent time period, hopefully a period beginning sometime after 1966. In that way, disclosure of bag jobs could be avoided, since J. Edgar Hoover had ordered the abandonment of the technique [they claim—L.S.] on July 19, 1966."

There is yet another feature of this document, which relates to a strange phenomenon about our case that we first noticed a few years ago. Key individuals in the FBI started dying. First, one or two. We didn't pay much attention to it. But it continued.

The most dramatic demise was that of William C. Sullivan. Beginning in 1961, Sullivan was the FBI's chief of "domestic intelligence," the man in overall command of all the operations against us and others. But he had a falling out with Hoover and retired from the FBI. After his forced retirement, he started talking—and he knew plenty. He told a congressional committee under oath that the FBI had not a single piece of evidence of any illegal actions committed by the SWP. He began doling out pieces of information to news reporters. He met privately on several occasions with Syd Stapleton, a leader of the SWP in charge of work on this suit. In 1977, Sullivan was shot to death in what was officially termed a "hunting accident." It's also known as "terminate with extreme prejudice."

This report turns up a few more bodies. And they die at the most interesting times. The investigators trace one very important meeting about our case to the White House, to the office of J. Fred Buzhardt. You may remember him from Watergate. He was Nixon's White House counsel. It turns out he was the only one who could answer a vital question. Buzhardt also had information, this report indicates, about a number of "bag jobs" against the SWP that took place after 1969, *three years after* the FBI supposedly stopped using this technique. But, the document reports, "approximately 48 hours before Buzhardt was to have been interviewed in this inquiry, he died suddenly."

This is, all in all, a true cover-up document. It ends up by blaming the deceased for all the wrongdoing, while the living are exonerated. But it does document a massive conspiracy to obstruct justice, and we will take this new opening and demand the full story, the whole truth.

The FBI has been caught in lie after lie about the burglaries. They have been lying about the wiretaps and the agents provocateurs. They have been lying about everything. It turns out that the files we have been given constitute just a tiny part of the real picture. We're not going to let this slide. We will pursue them on this, on the Heisler files and wherever else they may lead us, on the burglaries, on the cover-ups, everything going back to 1938 and right up to today.

Our campaign around this case will be a big asset in the next period. Because tied in with the militarization drive of the ruling class is their drive to strengthen the FBI and CIA. This campaign is already under way.

Just as the rulers must try to overcome the "Vietnam syndrome," they have got to overcome the widespread distrust of and opposition to the political police. Seizing on events from Iran to Jamaica, they try to convince American workers that the CIA and FBI are necessary to "national security" and should be strengthened. They have been pressing further bills in Congress to legalize and legitimize secret-police methods, and even to prosecute anyone who reveals the names of their agents.

As part of this, we are experiencing a general step-up in incidents of FBI-type harassment. These are things we haven't seen for a while, including spying and harassment on the job, not just by the FBI and the cops but also by private detective agencies.

We have to think about this, how we're going to respond to it. It is not going to stop. It will increase. But it doesn't follow that we ought to pull back, to become more cautious, or less bold. Not at all.

From time to time, in a union or in one coalition or another, we get red-baited. When that happens, we sometimes think we must have made a mistake; maybe we were too bold. Sometimes we do make mistakes. But we can't judge whether we're doing the correct things by whether the right-wingers go after us. Sometimes—often—we get red-baited because we're doing *exactly* the right things.

The same goes for the FBI. They will be going after us because we will be doing the right things. The ruling class doesn't like the fact that socialists are starting to have an impact inside the labor movement. Gov. Jerry Brown threw us off the ballot in California, not because we made a mistake or because we didn't demonstrate enough support, but because we demonstrated *too much* support. We are doing a lot of things right now that the cops and the CIA and the FBI don't like. And we will be doing more.

Confrontation in the Caribbean

They understand the confrontation that is shaping up in the Caribbean and Central America, just as we do. They understand, as we understand, how high the stakes are. They know that politics in this country is not separate from that confrontation. The class struggle here is part of it, is affected by it, and in turn will have a decisive impact on the outcome of the showdown between U.S. imperialism and the workers and farmers of Central America and the Caribbean.

The rulers know that what's going on in El Salvador, in Guatemala, in Honduras, and in Cuba, Grenada, and Nicaragua is part of what's going on here. And they know where we fit in. Exactly. They don't want to see a solidarity movement in the United States. They don't want to see an antidraft movement. They don't want to see a socialist campaign of education to explain to American working people why their future lies in friendship and support to the workers and farmers of other countries.

So the fact that we are running into stepped-up harassment—and what we have seen is nothing compared to what we are going to see from the cops—doesn't mean we will pull back one bit in our efforts to turn the party outward, to deepen our participation as socialists in the working-class struggles, to be more open on the job, to do more socialist petitioning and campaigning on the streets and at the plant gates, to keep driving to link arms with the Cubans and the Grenadians and the Nicaraguans and all other revolutionary leaderships around the world, to keep reaching out to the rebel youth in the plants, reaching out to the Black fighters in Miami's Liberty City, reaching out to the defiant antiwar, draft-age youth.

In driving ahead on all of this we will be driving ahead in our battle with the FBI. Because their whole objective is to make us stop doing these things.

This fight with the political police can be a tremendous advantage to us. It is attractive to young workers who, through their own experiences, are coming to know firsthand about the cops, agents provocateurs, labor spies, political frame-ups, and all the rest. Serious working people know that solving the problems facing the working class, facing the labor movement, facing the Black struggle, the Latino struggle, the women's movement, requires a new leadership. A new leadership that knows how to fight and isn't afraid to fight. That is why our campaign against the FBI will attract to our ranks those who are looking for a way to fight back.

They will see the YSA and the SWP as organizations that are not afraid to take on the FBI, that have the confidence to do it, and that know how to do it *effectively*. We are landing some blows, unprecedented blows, to the secret police and the government they serve. Many young fighters will see that a movement that can do that is a movement they will want to be part of.

Also from Pathfinder

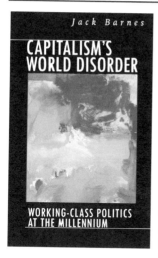

Capitalism's World Disorder

Working-Class Politics at the Millennium

JACK BARNES

The social devastation and financial panic, the coarsening of politics and politics of resentment, the cop brutality and acts of imperialist aggression accelerating around us—all are the product not of something gone wrong but of the lawful workings of capitalism. Yet the future can be changed by the united struggle and selfless action of workers and farmers conscious of their power to transform the world. $23.95

The Communist Manifesto

KARL MARX AND FREDERICK ENGELS

Founding document of the modern working-class movement, published in 1848. Explains why communism is derived not from preconceived principles but from facts and from proletarian movements springing from the actual class struggle. $3.95

To Speak the Truth

Why Washington's 'Cold War' against Cuba Doesn't End

FIDEL CASTRO AND CHE GUEVARA

In historic speeches before the United Nations and UN bodies, Guevara and Castro address the workers of the world, explaining why the U.S. government so hates the example set by the socialist revolution in Cuba and why Washington's effort to destroy it will fail. $16.95

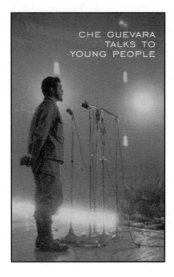

Che Guevara Talks to Young People

The legendary Argentine-born revolutionary challenges youth of Cuba and the world to read and to study. To work and become disciplined. To join the front lines of struggles, small and large. To read and to study. To aspire to be revolutionary combatants. To politicize their organizations and in the process politicize themselves. To become a different kind of human being as they strive together with working people of all lands to transform the world. And, along this line of march, to revel in the spontaneity and joy of being young. Also in Spanish. $14.95

Thomas Sankara Speaks

The Burkina Faso Revolution, 1983–87

Peasants and workers in the West African country of Burkina Faso established a popular revolutionary government and began to combat the hunger, illiteracy, and economic backwardness imposed by imperialist domination. Thomas Sankara, who led that struggle, explains the example set for all of Africa. $19.95

Genocide against the Indians

GEORGE NOVACK

Why did the leaders of the Europeans who settled in North America try to exterminate the peoples already living there? How was the campaign of genocide against the Indians linked to the expansion of capitalism in the United States? Noted Marxist George Novack answers these questions. $4.00

The Changing Face of U.S. Politics

Working-Class Politics and the Trade Unions

JACK BARNES

Building the kind of party the working class needs to prepare for coming class battles—battles through which they will revolutionize themselves, their unions, and all of society. It is a handbook for workers, farmers, and youth repelled by the social inequalities, economic instability, racism, women's oppression, cop violence, and wars endemic to capitalism...and who are determined to overturn that exploitative system and join in reconstructing the world on new, socialist foundations. $19.95

Teamster Rebellion

FARRELL DOBBS

The 1934 strikes that built the industrial union movement in Minneapolis and helped pave the way for the CIO, recounted by a central leader of that battle. The first in a four-volume series on the class-struggle leadership of the strikes and organizing drives that transformed the Teamsters union in much of the Midwest into a fighting social movement and pointed the road toward independent labor political action. $16.95

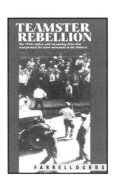

By Any Means Necessary

MALCOLM X

Speeches tracing the evolution of Malcolm X's views on political alliances, women's rights, intermarriage, capitalism and socialism, and more. $15.95

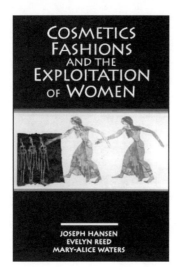

Cosmetics, Fashions, and the Exploitation of Women

JOSEPH HANSEN, EVELYN REED, AND MARY-ALICE WATERS

How big business plays on women's second-class status and social insecurities to market cosmetics and rake in profits. The introduction by Waters explains how the entry of millions of women into the workforce during and after World War II irreversibly changed U.S. society and laid the basis for a renewed rise of struggles for women's emancipation. $14.95

Making History

Interviews with Four Generals of Cuba's Revolutionary Armed Forces
Through the stories of four outstanding Cuban generals, each with close to half a century of revolutionary activity, we can see the class dynamics that have shaped our entire epoch. We can understand how the people of Cuba, as they struggle to build a new society, have for more than forty years held Washington at bay. Preface by Juan Almeida; introduction by Mary-Alice Waters. Also in Spanish. $15.95

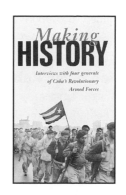

The History of the Russian Revolution

LEON TROTSKY

The social, economic, and political dynamics of the first socialist revolution as told by one of its central leaders. "The history of a revolution is for us first of all a history of the forcible entrance of the masses into the realm of rulership over their own destiny," Trotsky writes. Unabridged edition, 3 vols. in one. $35.95